Rediscover Church

Study Guide

Rediscover Church

Why the Body of Christ Is Essential

Study Guide

Collin Hansen and Jonathan Leeman

with Megan Hill

CROSSWAY®

WHEATON, ILLINOIS

SH-GR			29	28	27	26	25	24	23	22	21
14	13	12	11	10	9	8	7	6	5	4	3	2	1

Contents

Preface

AFTER A YEAR MARKED BY a global health crisis, political upheaval, and racial tension—in addition to the ordinary sins and stresses that press on every church in every year—Collin Hansen and Jonathan Leeman wrote *Rediscover Church* with the hope that weary and disconnected Christians would prioritize belonging to God's gathered people. The truths contained in their book are drawn from the ultimate source of truth, the Word of God, and the book was written so that pastors, members, and casual visitors would understand, as the subtitle says, *Why the Body of Christ Is Essential.*

This study guide is meant to help you as you consider the important place the church ought to have in your life. The quotations at the beginning of each section (noted with *RC*) are from the pages of *Rediscover Church*, and they invite you to think more deeply about key statements from Hansen and Leeman's book. Generally, those quotations are followed by related Scripture texts and questions designed to help you observe, interpret, and apply the Word of God to your own life as a part of Christ's church.

You may use this guide on your own, of course, but it will serve you best if you use it with others. When friends, discipleship groups, Sunday school classes, and even whole congregations gather to discuss the value of the body of Christ, the work of rediscovering church has already begun. As the Spirit convicts us, the Word compels us, and other Christians come alongside us, we will freshly encounter our need for the church—and we will renew our praise for the Savior who meets us there.

Megan Hill
August 2021

CHAPTER 1

What Is a Church?

Getting Started: "You may have many reasons not to go to church" (*RC*, p. 11). What things have kept you from going to church at times in the past? What has made you reluctant to attend in the previous year?

_____

_____

_____

_____

_____

1. Preaching and People

"If you had asked me in those days, 'What is a church?' I could not have given you a well-formed answer. But these two ideas of preaching and people—a gospel word and a gospel society—were growing in prominence in my mind. A church—I knew—has something to do with a group of people gathering to be shaped by God's Word." (*RC*, p. 23)

How has the Holy Spirit used preaching in your life? How has he used his people? Why are both preaching and people essential to what the church is?

_____

_____

_____

_____

_____

_____

_____

2. A Gospel Community

"More than anything else, your non-Christian friends need not just your gospel words but also a gospel community that testifies to the truth of those gospel words. You want them to watch the life of your church and say, 'God really does change people. And he really is building a just and righteous city—here in the church.'" (RC, p. 24)

Do you think of the ordinary life of the local church as inherently evangelistic? Why or why not? In what ways is gospel community attractive to non-Christians?

_____

_____

_____

_____

_____

_____

"For Zion's sake I will not keep silent, and for Jerusalem's sake I will not be quiet, until her righteousness goes forth as brightness, and her salvation as a burning torch. The nations shall see your righteousness, and all the kings your glory, and you shall be called by a new name that the mouth of the LORD will give. . . . And they shall be called The

Holy People, The Redeemed of the LORD; and you shall be called Sought Out, A City Not Forsaken." (Isa. 62:1–2, 12)

What does Isaiah say will be noticeable about the gathered people of God?

Who is going to see and seek out the city?

How are these verses being fulfilled in the church today? In what specific ways do the people in your community see righteousness and salvation displayed in your church?

---

3. Heaven Touching Earth

"Remarkably, amazingly, astoundingly, your church, the one we want you to rediscover, is the place where the Bible says heaven has begun to descend to earth. . . . Heaven touches down on planet earth through our gathered churches. And when this happens, you offer the citizens of your nation the hope of a better nation, the residents of your city the hope of a better and lasting city." (RC, p. 24–25)

Just as an embassy or colony is a small part of one kingdom established in another place, our local churches are heavenly territory on earth. In what ways is the surrounding culture different from life inside the church? Describe a time when you experienced heavenly realities in your local church.

_____

_____

_____

_____

_____

"But you have come to Mount Zion and to the city of the living God, the heavenly Jerusalem, and to innumerable angels in festal gathering, and to the assembly of the firstborn who are enrolled in heaven, and to God, the judge of all, and to the spirits of the righteous made perfect, and to Jesus, the mediator of a new covenant, and to the sprinkled blood that speaks a better word than the blood of Abel." (Heb. 12:22–24)

In these verses, the writer of the letter to the Hebrews describes the gathered worship of the church. What is your impression of worship after reading this text?

_____

_____

_____

_____

Puritan Matthew Henry divides these verses into "heavenly places" and "heavenly so-ciety" (Matthew Henry, *Matthew Henry's Commentary*, vol. 6, *Acts to Revelation* [1710; repr., Peabody, MA: Hendrickson, 1991], 772). Which words describe the place of worship? Which words describe the society in which we worship?

_____

_____

_____

_____

How would it change your experience on Sunday if you remembered that you are worship-ing in "the heavenly Jerusalem"? How would it change your experience if you remembered that you are worshiping alongside the whole host of heaven? How would it change your experience if you remembered you are worshiping in the company of Jesus himself?

_____

_____

_____

_____

Are you eager to invite your non-Christian friends and neighbors to your church? Why or why not? Would you be more eager if you believed you were inviting them to participate in heavenly worship?

_____

_____

_____

_____

_____

4. What Is a Church?

Look over the graphic on the opposite page. Which parts of this definition of a church are statements you expected? Which parts are new or surprising to you?

_____

_____

_____

_____

Which parts of the definition raise questions or objections in your mind? Make a list of your questions and look for the answers as you work through the following chapters.

A church is a group of Christians (chapter 2)

↓

who assemble as an earthly embassy of
Christ's heavenly kingdom (chapter 3)

↓

to proclaim the good news and
commands of Christ the King (chapter 4);

↓

to affirm one another as his citizens
through the ordinances (chapter 5);

↓

and to display God's own
holiness and love (chapter 6)

↓

through a unified and
diverse people (chapter 7)

↓

in all the world (chapter 8),

↓

following the teaching and
example of elders (chapter 9).

5. Loved and Loving One Another

"What is a church? It's a group of people who know they've been loved by Christ and have begun to love one another like that." (*RC*, p. 28)

In what ways have you experienced Christlike love in the church? In what ways do you seek to show Christlike love to others?

_____

_____

_____

_____

"In this is love, not that we have loved God but that he loved us and sent his Son to be the propitiation for our sins. Beloved, if God so loved us, we also ought to love one another. No one has ever seen God; if we love one another, God abides in us and his love is perfected in us." (1 John 4:10–12)

How did God demonstrate his love toward us?

_____

_____

_____

_____

What is the basis of our love for other Christians? Is this love optional? What words does John use to stress the importance of loving one another in the church?

_____

_____

_____

_____

_____

Sometimes it's difficult to love other Christians in the church—they can be awkward, abrasive, or even hurtful. What encouragement do these verses offer us?

_____

_____

_____

_____

CHAPTER 2

Who Can Belong to a Church?

Getting Started: In a few sentences, tell your story of coming to faith in Christ.

_____

_____

_____

_____

_____

_____

1. By Birth or Adoption

"Earlier we likened the church to a spiritual family. What does that mean? To become a part of a family, you need to be either born or adopted. And the Bible actually uses both concepts to describe what's called conversion, which is how you become part of this spiritual family of the church. Just as you don't choose to be born or adopted, so also you don't choose conversion." (*RC*, p. 34)

You didn't choose your parents or siblings, and you don't choose to be part of God's family either. How does this truth humble you?

_____

_____

"Once you were not a people, but now you are God's people; once you had not received mercy, but now you have received mercy." (1 Pet. 2:10)

Before our conversion, what two things were true of us? What is different since our conversion?

_____

_____

_____

What does this verse teach us about the corporate nature of salvation?

_____

_____

What do adopted children receive from their adoptive parents? In what ways is conversion similar to adoption?

_____

_____

_____

_____

2. Born of Water and Spirit

"Who can visit a church building for a worship service? The answer is, anyone! But who can belong to the spiritual family called the church? Only those who have entered the kingdom of God. Only those who have been born of water and the Spirit, according to Jesus—that is, only those who have been born again and been baptized." (RC, p. 35)

Many church buildings display a sign that reads, "All Are Welcome." In what way is this statement true? In what way could it be misleading?

_____

_____

_____

_____

_____

"To all those in Rome who are loved by God and called to be saints . . ." (Rom. 1:7a)

"To the church of God that is in Corinth, to those sanctified in Christ Jesus, called to be saints together with all those who in every place call upon the name of our Lord Jesus Christ, both their Lord and ours . . ." (1 Cor. 1:2)

"To the saints who are in Ephesus, and are faithful in Christ Jesus . . ." (Eph. 1:1b)

"To the saints and faithful brothers in Christ at Colossae . . ." (Col. 1:2a)

Each of these verses is Paul's greeting to a particular first-century church. What words does he use to describe the people of those congregations?

_____

_____

_____

How were the people in these congregations different from the rest of the people who lived in Rome, Corinth, Ephesus, and Colossae?

_____

_____

_____

_____

If Paul were writing to your local church, how might he describe the members?

_____

_____

_____

_____

3. Gathered to Worship

"To rediscover church is to realize or remember why we gather in the first place. We gather to worship God—Father, Son, and Holy Spirit—who has saved us from sin and death. That's what we sing. That's what we teach. That's what we observe in baptism and the Lord's Supper.

Without conversion, without being born again, there is no church to rediscover. If Jesus has not died for our sins and been raised on the third day, there is no more hope to be found inside the church than outside." (RC, p. 37)

What is the essential activity of the gathered church? What is the essential content of that activity? What is the essential hope the church professes?

_____

_____

_____

_____

_____

_____

What do the authors mean when they say "Without conversion, without being born again, there is no church to rediscover"?

_____

_____

_____

_____

_____

"And you were dead in the trespasses and sins in which you once walked, following the course of this world, following the prince of the power of the air, the spirit that is now at work in the sons of disobedience—among whom we all once lived in the passions of our flesh, carrying out the desires of the body and the mind, and were by nature children of wrath, like the rest of mankind. But God, being rich in mercy, because of the great love with which he loved us, even when we were dead in our trespasses, made us alive together with Christ—by grace you have been saved—and raised us up with him and seated us with him in the heavenly places in Christ Jesus, so that in the coming ages he might show the immeasurable riches of his grace in kindness toward us in Christ Jesus." (Eph. 2:1–7)

These verses divide the believer's life into two parts: first, we are dead in sin, then we are alive with Christ. Which words describe people before conversion? Which words describe believers after conversion? Who is the agent of change in every believer's life (see v. 4)?

_____

_____

_____

_____

_____

_____

It's not pleasant to consider our lives before conversion, but Paul doesn't look away. Why do you think it's important for believers to acknowledge what we once were? Why do you think it's important to affirm that all of us in the church were once "children of wrath"?

_____

_____

_____

_____

How did your conversion change you?

_____

_____

_____

_____

_____

4. Personal and Corporate

"Conversion can happen inside or outside the church. It can be a solitary experience or one you share with friends and peers. But it should always result in you linking together with a church." (RC, p. 38)

In what ways is conversion a personal experience? In what ways does it have corporate implications?

_____

_____

_____

_____

"But Ruth said, 'Do not urge me to leave you or to return from following you. For where you go I will go, and where you lodge I will lodge. Your people shall be my people, and your God my God.'" (Ruth 1:16)

The Lord worked in the heart of Ruth through the testimony of her believing mother-in-law, Naomi. How did Ruth's allegiances change as a result of her conversion?

_____

_____

_____

_____

"So those who received his word were baptized, and there were added that day about three thousand souls. . . . And the Lord added to their number day by day those who were being saved." (Acts 2:41, 47b)

The Lord worked in the hearts of many citizens of first-century Jerusalem through the preaching of the apostles and the testimony of the church. What does Luke mean when he says that these new converts were "added"?

_____

_____

_____

Think of the stories of a few Old and New Testament saints. Did any of them live the life of faith in solitude? How could you use these examples to encourage someone who is reluctant to join a church?

_____

_____

_____

_____

5. Set Apart

"If you've been born again, if you have repented of your sins and believe in Jesus, you can belong to the church." (RC, pp. 41–42)

What is necessary in order to join the church? What things do people sometimes *think* are necessary but aren't?

_____

_____

_____

_____

_____

_____

What is the process for joining your local church?

_____

_____

_____

_____

How do the truths in this chapter encourage you to commit—or recommit—yourself to Christ and his church?

_____

_____

_____

_____

CHAPTER 3

Do We Really Need to Gather?

Getting Started: Reflect on a time when you were unable to gather with the church and had to participate virtually via livestream. What did you miss most?

_____

_____

_____

_____

_____

1. The Power of Gathering

"What makes gatherings so powerful? The fact that you are physically there. You see. You hear. You feel. Unlike watching something on a screen, in which you're bodily removed from the thing you're watching, a gathering literally surrounds you. It defines your entire reality. . . . In a gathering, we experience what other people love, hate, fear, and believe, and our sense of what's normal and what's right can shift comparatively quickly. The loves, hates, fears, or beliefs of the crowd become ours." (RC, p. 46)

Think of a gathering you attended that made an impression on you. Maybe it was a concert, a rally, or even a dinner party in someone's home. How did the other people at the gathering influence you? Why would your experience have been different if you had watched the event from home on a screen?

_____

_____

_____

_____

_____

In what ways have you been shaped by the people in your church? How would their impact have been lessened if you had never spent time with them in person?

_____

_____

_____

_____

2. Churches Gather and Are Gatherings

"Sometimes people like to say that 'a church is a people, not a place.' It's slightly more accurate to say that a church is a people assembled in a place. Regularly assembling or gathering makes a church a church. This doesn't mean a church stops being a church when the people aren't gathered, any more than a soccer 'team' stops being a team when the members are not playing. The point is, regularly gathering together is necessary for a church to be a church, just like a team has to gather to play in order to be a team." (RC, p. 48)

What objections have you heard (or held) to the assertion that a church must gather in order to be a church? How does the above sports team analogy help to answer those objections?

_____

_____

_____

_____

_____

_____

"The churches of Asia send you greetings. Aquila and Prisca, together with the church in their house, send you hearty greetings in the Lord." (1 Cor. 16:19)

"Give my greetings to the brothers at Laodicea, and to Nympha and the church in her house." (Col. 4:15)

What words in these verses highlight the fact that the church is a people? What words highlight the fact that the church always assembles in a place?

_____

_____

_____

_____

How do the details in these verses encourage us to think of the church in concrete and local terms (rather than simply as an abstract idea)?

_____

_____

_____

_____

"And let us consider how to stir up one another to love and good works, not neglecting to meet together, as is the habit of some, but encouraging one another, and all the more as you see the Day drawing near." (Heb. 10:24–25)

What does the writer of the letter to the Hebrews warn the people against neglecting?

According to these verses, what benefits do we give and receive when we meet together?

Why should Christ's return ("the Day drawing near") compel us to gather as a church? What are some ways we encourage one another in the church in light of Christ's return?

3. The Church Cannot Be Downloaded

"Think about it. Maybe you struggle with hidden hatred toward a brother all week. But then his presence at the Lord's Table draws you to conviction and confession. You struggle with suspicion toward a sister. But then you see her singing the same songs of praise, and your heart warms. You struggle with anxiety over what's happening politically in your nation. But then the preacher declares Christ's coming in victory and vindication, you hear shouts of 'Amen!' all around you, and you recall that you belong to a heavenly citizenry allied in hope. You're tempted to keep your struggle in the dark. But then the older couple's tender but pressing question over lunch—'How are you really?'—*draws you into the light.*

None of this can be experienced virtually. God made us physical and relational creatures. The Christian life and the church life cannot finally be downloaded. It must be watched, heard, stepped into, and followed." (RC, p. 52)

What are some of the hidden struggles we experience in the Christian life? How does the presence of other believers in the church help us to fight our sin, reorient our perspective, and overcome our doubts?

_____

_____

_____

_____

_____

"Therefore when we could bear it no longer, we were willing to be left behind at Athens alone, and we sent Timothy, our brother and God's coworker in the gospel of Christ, to establish and exhort you in your faith, that no one be moved by these afflictions. . . . For what thanksgiving can we return to God for you, for all the joy that we feel for your sake

before our God, as we pray most earnestly night and day that we may see you face to face and supply what is lacking in your faith?" (1 Thess. 3:1–3a, 9–10)

How would you describe Paul's feelings toward the Thessalonian church?

_____

_____

_____

_____

When Paul became concerned about the Thessalonians' spiritual struggles, what did he do (vv. 1–3)? What did he constantly pray for (v. 10)?

_____

_____

_____

_____

Why do you think Paul wasn't content to simply write to the Thessalonians from afar? What is the connection between loving someone and wanting to be physically present with them? What is the connection between helping someone and taking steps to be physically present with them?

_____

_____

_____

How do these verses encourage you to gather with the local church?

4. Overcoming an Autonomous Mindset

"[To] offer or encourage the virtual church as a permanent option, even with good intentions, hurts Christian discipleship. It trains Christians to think of their faith in autonomous terms. It teaches them that they can follow Jesus as a member of the 'family of God,' in some abstract sense, without teaching them what it means to be a part of a family and to make sacrifices for a family." (RC, p. 53)

It's common for people in the West to assume that faith can flourish apart from other believers. Maybe you've made such an assumption yourself. What are some examples of this kind of thinking?

How is "the push toward virtual church" a "push to individualize Christianity" (*RC*, p. 53)?

_____

_____

_____

_____

_____

"And all who believed were together and had all things in common." (Acts 2:44)

What three things characterized the early church, according to this verse?

_____

_____

_____

How does this verse contrast with the contemporary view of faith as private and individual?

_____

_____

_____

_____

_____

In what ways has gathering with the church forced you to hold loosely to your own preferences, priorities, and possessions? How has this sometimes been challenging? How has it been a blessing?

_____

_____

_____

_____

_____

_____

5. An Embassy of Heaven

"What's a gathered church? It's an embassy of heaven. Step inside your church or ours, and what should you find? A whole different nation—sojourners, exiles, citizens of Christ's kingdom. Inside such churches, you'll hear the King of heaven's words declared. You'll hear heaven's language of faith, hope, and love. You'll get a taste of the end-time heavenly banquet through the Lord's Supper. And you'll be charged with its diplomatic business as you're called to bring the gospel to your nation and every other nation." (RC, p. 54)

If the church is a nation—or an embassy of a nation—who is its ruler? What are its laws? What is its mission in the world? Who are its citizens?

_____

_____

_____

_____

_____

_____

_____

What implications does heavenly citizenship have for your life?

_____

_____

_____

_____

CHAPTER 4

Why Are Preaching and Teaching Central?

Getting Started: In a typical week, where do you hear messages of human wisdom? What is appealing about your favorite podcasts, audiobooks, radio shows, or YouTube channels?

_____

_____

_____

_____

_____

_____

1. Hearing from the Divine King

"We get up and gather with the church weekly because that's where we hear from the divine King—his good news and his counsel for our lives. We hear from him every time we open our Bibles, yes, but we hear from him together in the weekly gathering. We're shaped together as a people there. This is why preaching and teaching are central to our church gatherings. Centering our gatherings around God's Word cultivates the heavenly culture that should characterize us as a distinct people, so that we can, in turn, be salt and light in our separate cities and nations." (RC, p. 59)

Collin Hansen writes, "As we rediscover church, we're looking for divine authority and not merely human wisdom" (*RC*, p. 58). In contrast to the many sources of human wisdom we discussed earlier, where is the only place to find the trustworthy revelation of divine truth?

_____

_____

_____

_____

Why should we prioritize God's Word in our lives? Why do we need to hear it together as a church?

_____

_____

_____

_____

_____

"[Jesus said,] 'But the hour is coming, and is now here, when the true worshipers will worship the Father in spirit and truth, for the Father is seeking such people to worship him. God is spirit, and those who worship him must worship in spirit and truth.'" (John 4:23–24)

What two things are necessary for true worship?

_____

_____

_____

Who is the Spirit? How does the Spirit help us to worship? How do we get the Spirit's help?

_____

_____

_____

_____

_____

_____

Who reveals truth to us? Where do we find this truth? Why is truth the basis for our worship?

_____

_____

_____

_____

_____

_____

Worship in our local churches will generally be unappealing to someone who is not filled with the Spirit and a lover of God's Word. Can you think of a time when Word-centered worship seemed boring or offensive to you? How can you grow in love for the Spirit and truth?

_____

_____

_____

_____

_____

_____

_____

2. Showing God's Glory

"The best preachers don't make you marvel at their own skill. They show you God's glory as seen in his Word. And when you see God that way, you want as much of him as you can get. You grow in eagerness to read and apply the Word for yourself. Then you enter a virtuous feedback loop. The more preachers help you know and love the Word, the more you develop that taste for yourself, and the better taste you develop for meaty preaching." (*RC*, pp. 61–62)

Why is it tempting to seek out a preacher who tells you what you want to hear? Why is it tempting to prioritize a preacher's giftedness or relatability over his commitment to God's Word? How does the availability of online resources contribute to this temptation?

_____

_____

_____

_____

_____

_____

"When [Jesus] went ashore he saw a great crowd, and he had compassion on them, because they were like sheep without a shepherd. And he began to teach them many things." (Mark 6:34)

How did Jesus feel toward the crowd?

What analogy does Mark use to describe the people's problem? What did Jesus do in response?

Sheep are largely helpless. They need a shepherd to give them food, direct them where to go, and keep them safe from danger. Why is this more important to the sheep than having a shepherd who is entertaining or a shepherd who simply does what the sheep want? How does a faithful preacher feed, guide, and protect the congregation when he preaches God's Word?

_____

_____

Think of a time when you were shepherded well by a preacher who taught you God's Word. How did his ministry cause you to love God's Word more?

_____

_____

_____

_____

3. Four Movements

"Think about the work of the Word in a church through at least four movements: (1) the preacher brings the Word for the whole church; (2) the church members respond by taking God's Word into their mouths and hearts through the singing and corporate prayers; (3) all members of the church teach the Word to themselves; and (4) various members of the church teach the Word to one another and to the next generation." (RC, p. 62)

In any given week in your church, where and when do each of these things happen? Which of these are regular parts of your life? In what areas do you need to renew your commitment to receiving and/or teaching God's Word?

_____

_____

_____

_____

4. A Communal Event

"Two things happen with live, in-person teaching that can't be replicated on a podcast with a pastor you'll never know personally. First, the congregation and the preacher together experience preaching as a communal event in time and space. . . . The sermon casts a vision from God's Word for a particular people in a particular place, as they have covenanted together to obey God and love one another." (RC, pp. 66–67)

"And [Ezra] read from [the Book of the Law] facing the square before the Water Gate from early morning until midday, in the presence of the men and the women and those who could understand. And the ears of all the people were attentive to the Book of the Law. . . . Also [the Levites] helped the people to understand the Law, while the people remained in their places. They read from the book, from the Law of God, clearly, and they gave the sense, so that the people understood the reading. . . . And all the people went their way to eat and drink and to send portions and to make great rejoicing, because they had understood the words that were declared to them." (Neh. 8:3, 7–8, 12)

What did Ezra read aloud? Who was present in the gathering? What did the Levites do? How did the people respond?

_____

_____

_____

_____

How are reading, hearing, explaining, understanding, responding, and rejoicing connected in this passage? In what ways do you see these connections in your own church's worship service?

_____

_____

_____

_____

_____

How would this story have been different if Ezra, the Levites, and the people had not been physically present with one another? How does this passage encourage you to be present when God's Word is preached and taught?

_____

_____

_____

_____

_____

5. Changed Hearers

"Second, the preacher's example and personality set a tone for the whole congregation. . . . The preacher's character and message meld together, and, by the power of the Spirit, hearers are changed by those words, even if they don't always remember them. And that's common for teaching, not just preaching. We don't typically remember our best teachers just for their knowledge. We remember their wisdom alongside their gifting to communicate and their love for us personally." (RC, p. 67)

Think of a teacher from your childhood who was especially influential in your early life. What made that person such an effective teacher?

_____

_____

_____

_____

"Let no one despise you for your youth, but set the believers an example in speech, in conduct, in love, in faith, in purity. Until I come, devote yourself to the public reading of Scripture, to exhortation, to teaching." (1 Tim. 4:12–13)

In these verses, seasoned pastor Paul gives instructions to younger pastor Timothy. Which of his instructions concern Timothy's character? Which of his instructions concern Timothy's teaching and preaching?

_____

_____

_____

In what way are the preacher's character and gifts inextricably connected to his work of preaching God's Word?

_____

_____

_____

_____

_____

What does this mean for what we should look for in a pastor?

_____

_____

_____

_____

_____

CHAPTER 5

Is Joining Actually Necessary?

Getting Started: List the authorities in your life. Over what sphere (or area) does each exercise authority? In what ways have you seen the blessing of being under authority? In what ways is it sometimes difficult to see?

_____

_____

_____

_____

_____

_____

1. Church Authority

> *"The authority of the keys = the right to declare on*
> *Jesus's behalf the* what *and the* who *of the gospel:*
> *What is a right confession? Who is a true confessor?"* (RC, p. 73)

Which two things does the church declare? On whose behalf does it make this declaration? In what ways is the church's job like that of a courtroom judge?

_____

_____

_____

_____

_____

_____

2. The Ordinances: Heavenly Passports

"Too often, Christians treat the ordinances individualistically. We practice baptism and the Supper at home, at camp, or on overseas tours. Remaining at home through COVID-19 especially tempted people to think this way. . . .

Yet the normal practice is to celebrate these two ordinances within the church gathering under the church's watchful care, as when three thousand were baptized 'into' the Jerusalem church (Acts 2:41). Likewise, Paul warns us to participate in the Supper only while 'discerning the body,' meaning the church (1 Cor. 11:29). Then he tells us to 'wait for one another' before taking it (v. 33). This is a church event." (RC, pp. 74–75)

When have you seen (or heard of) baptism or the Lord's Supper practiced apart from the local church?

_____

_____

_____

What would you tell someone who believes the ordinances can be administered among individuals or nonchurch groups?

_____

_____

_____

_____

_____

"When you come together, it is not the Lord's supper that you eat. For in eating, each one goes ahead with his own meal. One goes hungry, another gets drunk. What! Do you not have houses to eat and drink in? Or do you despise the church of God and humiliate those who have nothing? What shall I say to you? Shall I commend you in this? No, I will not. . . . So then, my brothers, when you come together to eat, wait for one another—if anyone is hungry, let him eat at home—so that when you come together it will not be for judgment." (1 Cor. 11:20–22, 33–34a)

What were the Corinthian believers doing wrong? Describe what their meal was like. What does Paul say their individualistic and chaotic meal was *not*?

_____

_____

_____

_____

Twice Paul says, "when you come together" (vv. 20, 33). What assumption about the context of the Lord's Supper is Paul making? What other words in this passage place the right practice of the Lord's Supper in the church gathering?

_____

_____

_____

_____

_____

_____

✦ The next time you participate in the Lord's Supper, what are some things you could do to remind yourself that it's a family meal?

_____

_____

_____

_____

3. What Is Church Membership?

"Church membership is how we formally recognize and commit to one another as believers. It's the thing we create by affirming one another through the ordinances. To offer a definition, church membership is a church's affirmation *and* oversight *of a Christian's profession of faith and discipleship, combined with the Christian's* submission *to the church and its oversight."* (*RC*, p. 75)

What does Jonathan Leeman mean by *affirmation*? What does he mean by *oversight*? In what ways does your local church do each of those things?

_____

_____

_____

_____

_____

What does he mean by *submission*? In what ways do the members of your local church submit to the church?

_____

_____

_____

_____

_____

_____

"So I exhort the elders among you, as a fellow elder and a witness of the sufferings of Christ, as well as a partaker in the glory that is going to be revealed: shepherd the flock of God that is among you, exercising oversight, not under compulsion, but willingly, as God would have you; not for shameful gain, but eagerly; not domineering over those in your charge, but being examples to the flock. And when the chief Shepherd appears, you will receive the unfading crown of glory. Likewise, you who are younger, be subject to the elders. Clothe yourselves, all of you, with humility toward one another, for 'God opposes the proud but gives grace to the humble.'" (1 Pet. 5:1–5)

According to these verses, who is the ultimate authority in the church? (Hint: it's not the elders.)

_____

_____

_____

What three groups does Peter instruct? What does he tell each group to do?

_____

_____

_____

_____

_____

_____

Who do elders submit to? Who do the "younger" submit to? Who should everyone submit to (cf. Eph. 5:21)?

_____

_____

_____

_____

_____

When have you seen gracious oversight practiced in your church?

_____

_____

_____

_____

When have you seen humble submission practiced in your church?

_____

_____

_____

_____

_____

4. Is Belonging to the Universal Church Enough?

"Sometimes people like to say, 'I don't need to join a church. I already belong to Christ's universal church.'" (RC, p. 76)

In what ways is this statement true? In what ways is it false? What would you say to someone making this claim?

_____

_____

_____

_____

_____

"Another question people ask is whether church membership is even in the Bible. Maybe you've asked it yourself." (RC, p. 78)

In what sense is the answer to this question no? In what sense is the answer yes? What would you say to someone asking this question?

_____

_____

_____

_____

_____

_____

"Greet Prisca and Aquila, my fellow workers in Christ Jesus, who risked their necks for my life, to whom not only I give thanks but all the churches of the Gentiles give thanks as well. Greet also the church in their house. Greet my beloved Epaenetus, who was the first convert to Christ in Asia. Greet Mary, who has worked hard for you. Greet Adronicus and Junia, my kinsmen and my fellow prisoners. They are well known to the apostles, and they were in Christ before me. Greet Ampliatus, my beloved in the Lord. Greet Urbanus, our fellow worker in Christ, and my beloved Stachys. Greet Appelles, who is approved in Christ. Greet those who belong to the family of Aristobulus. Greet my kinsman Herodion. Greet those in the Lord who belong to the family of Narcissus. Greet those workers in the Lord, Tryphaena and Tryphosa. Greet the beloved Persis, who has worked hard in the Lord. Greet Rufus, chosen in the Lord; also his mother, who has been a mother to me as well. Greet Asyncritus, Phlegon, Hermes, Patrobas, Hermas, and the brothers who are with them. Greet Philologus, Julia, Nereus and his sister, and Olympas, and all the saints who are with them. Greet one another with a holy kiss. All the churches of Christ greet you." (Rom. 16:3–16)

What is this passage about?

_____

_____

_____

_____

_____

Choose one of the names from this passage. What can we assume about that person simply from his or her inclusion in these verses? What unique details does Paul give about that person?

_____

_____

_____

_____

Why do you think Paul chose to name church members rather than simply offering a general greeting? Why do you think the Lord included this list of specific names in Holy Scripture?

_____

_____

_____

_____

How does a passage like this one help us to understand whether membership in a local church is biblical? How does it help us to understand whether membership in a local church is important?

_____

_____

_____

_____

5. Membership Is a Job

"The big takeaway for you right now is that church membership is not a passive thing. It's not just a status. It's not like membership in a country club, a shopper's club, or a gas station rewards program. It's a job where you go to work. You need to get job training. You need to engage it with your mind and heart. You need to think about making an impact. What are you going to produce this week? Are you benefiting the whole team and carrying your weight or are you slacking off?" (RC, p. 83)

Which community organizations do you participate in? What are the differences between belonging to a club and being employed at your workplace?

_____

_____

_____

_____

If belonging to the church is a job, who is your boss? Who are your coworkers? What are your responsibilities? What are your hours? How do you get job training? What should be your attitude as you work?

_____

_____

_____

_____

_____

_____

Skim Romans 16:3–16, above. What are some of the contributions to the church that Paul describes?

_____

_____

_____

_____

Notice the variety of people listed. Can you find mention of a man? A woman? An older person? A family? What does this tell you about the nature of the church?

_____

_____

_____

_____

_____

If Paul had included you in his list of greetings, what words might he have used to describe your contribution to the church? In the weeks and years to come, what would you like your legacy in the church to include?

_____

_____

_____

_____

CHAPTER 6

Is Church Discipline Really Loving?

Getting Started: Think of a time when someone—perhaps a teacher, coach, or employer—corrected you when you were getting something wrong. How was that experience uncomfortable? How was it helpful?

_____

_____

_____

_____

_____

_____

_____

1. Correcting Sin

"Making Christian disciples involves teaching and correcting, and people use the term 'church discipline' to mean the second part—correcting sin. The discipline process begins with private warnings. . . . The process ends either when a person repents or, if necessary, when the church removes the unrepentant person from church membership and participation in the Lord's Table." (*RC*, pp. 87–88)

Do you think of church discipline as negative or positive? Why?

_____

_____

_____

_____

_____

Do you think of it as a process or a single action? Why?

_____

_____

_____

_____

Why is it important that discipleship (and discipline) happens in the context of ongoing relationships?

_____

_____

_____

_____

_____

What is the process for church discipline in your local church?

_____

_____

_____

_____

_____

2. A Biblical Process

"First, is church discipline really in the Bible? Yes." (RC, p. 91)

Who is ultimately in charge of the church?

_____

_____

_____

_____

Why is Jonathan Leeman's question above vital for churches to ask and answer?

_____

_____

_____

_____

"If your brother sins against you, go and tell him his fault, between you and him alone. If he listens to you, you have gained your brother. But if he does not listen, take one or two others along with you, that every charge may be established by the evidence of two or three

witnesses. If he refuses to listen to them, tell it to the church. And if he refuses to listen even to the church, let him be to you as a Gentile and a tax collector." (Matt. 18:15–17)

What is the problem that begins the church discipline process (v. 15)? What kinds of things are *not* grounds for church discipline? What kinds of things are?

List the steps of the process Jesus describes. What causes the process to move from one step to the next?

What does Jesus mean when he tells the church to view an unrepentant person as "a Gentile and a tax collector"? What was the spiritual condition of Gentiles and tax collectors? What would it look like for Jesus's hearers to treat someone as a Gentile or a tax collector?

_____

_____

_____

_____

How should we relate to a person who persists in sin after being disciplined by the church?

_____

_____

_____

_____

_____

"When you are assembled in the name of the Lord Jesus and my spirit is present, with the power of our Lord Jesus, you are to deliver this [unrepentant, sexually immoral] man to Satan for the destruction of the flesh, so that his spirit may be saved in the day of the Lord. Your boasting is not good. Do you not know that a little leaven leavens the whole lump? Cleanse out the old leaven that you may be a new lump, as you really are unleavened. For Christ, our Passover lamb, has been sacrificed." (1 Cor. 5:4–7)

What problem required the Corinthian church to practice discipline (see 1 Cor. 5:1–2)?

_____

_____

_____

What did Paul instruct the Corinthians to do (vv. 4–5; cf. v. 2)?

_____

_____

_____

_____

What are the goals of church discipline (vv. 5, 7)?

_____

_____

_____

_____

You may know someone who thinks church discipline seems arrogant ("Who are we to judge someone else?"), but, interestingly, Paul describes the *failure* to eradicate sin as "boasting" (v. 6). What would you say to someone who equates church discipline with pride?

_____

_____

_____

_____

How does this passage help you understand the necessity of the difficult, uncomfortable process of church discipline for the good of the whole church?

_____

_____

_____

_____

_____

3. Discipline for Love's Sake

"Fundamentally, then, churches should practice church discipline for love's sake:
- *love for the sinner's sake, that he or she might come to repentance;*
- *love for the other church members' sake, that they might not be led astray;*
- *love for the non-Christian neighbors' sake, that they might not just see more worldliness in the church; and*
- *love for Christ's sake, that we might represent his name rightly."* (RC, pp. 95–96)

Think of a time when someone—a pastor, a mentor, a friend—in the church corrected you for sin. How was that experience hard? How was it ultimately good for your soul?

_____

_____

_____

_____

_____

Have you ever corrected someone else who was caught in sin? In what ways was it difficult? What did you learn from that experience?

_____

_____

_____

_____

How does thinking of church discipline as a loving act impact the way we receive rebukes from fellow believers? How does it impact the way we approach a brother or sister caught in sin?

_____

_____

_____

_____

Sadly, sometimes church discipline has no effect on the sinner's heart. In those situations, how does remembering that discipline has loving purposes beyond just that person encourage you?

_____

_____

_____

4. God's Holy Love

"There's one specific thing about God's love that church discipline teaches us, and it is so often missing from definitions: God's love is holy. You can't have God's love apart from his holiness. His love serves his holy purposes, and his holy purposes are loving. Sometimes people pit so-called 'holiness churches' against 'loving churches.' That's impossible. A church must be both of those or it is neither of them." (RC, p. 96)

Do you tend to value love or holiness more? Why?

_____

_____

_____

_____

Why do love and holiness sometimes seem incompatible? What cultural messages reinforce that perception?

_____

_____

_____

_____

_____

"As obedient children, do not be conformed to the passions of your former ignorance, but as he who called you is holy, you also be holy in all your conduct, since it is written, 'You shall be holy, for I am holy.'" (1 Pet. 1:14–16)

What does Peter call believers? Why do you think he uses family language?

_____

_____

_____

_____

What is believers' motivation to forsake sin and pursue righteousness?

_____

_____

_____

How is God's holiness and just judgment a comfort to someone who is being mistreated?

_____

_____

_____

_____

How does insisting on holiness in the church reflect the character of God in the family of God? How does it protect the vulnerable from abuse and exploitation?

_____

_____

_____

_____

_____

_____

Why would it be *un*loving to encourage someone to join a church where abusive and wicked people were never disciplined?

_____

_____

_____

5. Knowing and Being Known

"What's the takeaway in all of this for you? Make sure you're building relationships with other members of the church so that you can know them and they can know you. Trust grows in an environment of conversational humility and honesty. Work to be the kind of person who is easy to correct." (RC, p. 99)

Are you easy to correct? Explain.

_____

_____

_____

_____

_____

"But when Cephas [Peter] came to Antioch, I opposed him to his face, because he stood condemned. For before certain men came from James, he was eating with the Gentiles; but when they came he drew back and separated himself, fearing the circumcision party. And the rest of the Jews acted hypocritically along with him, so that even Barnabas was led astray by their hypocrisy. But when I saw that their conduct was not in step with the truth of the gospel, I said to Cephas before them all, 'If you, though a Jew, live like a Gentile and not like a Jew, how can you force the Gentiles to live like Jews?'" (Gal. 2:11–14)

What was Peter doing? Why?

_____

_____

_____

_____

What impact did it have on the other believers?

_____

_____

_____

_____

How did Paul respond? Based on the details he gives in this passage, what do you think motivated him to speak up?

_____

_____

_____

_____

_____

How might this situation have been different if Paul and Peter had not already established mutual love and respect for one another?

_____

_____

_____

_____

_____

In what areas do you need to be more like Paul: willing to speak up for the good of others when the gospel is at stake?

_____

_____

_____

_____

_____

In what areas do you need to be more like Peter: willing to hear and receive the rebukes of other believers?

_____

_____

_____

_____

"Search me, O God, and know my heart!
   Try me and know my thoughts!
And see if there be any grievous way in me,
   and lead me in the way everlasting!" (Ps. 139:23–24)

What is the psalmist's desire? Is this your desire?

_____

_____

_____

_____

In what ways does the Lord use his church as his instrument to search, try, know, and lead you?

_____

_____

_____

_____

CHAPTER 7

How Do I Love Members Who Are Different?

Getting Started: Think about a relationship you have in the church with someone who is different from you. Maybe that person is a different age, from a different educational background, or of a different race. In what ways has that relationship been a blessing to you?

_____

_____

_____

_____

_____

1. The Comfort of the Familiar

"This exercise gives you a window into how many church leaders today think. We started with the stated goal of numeric growth. But did you catch the underlying assumption in all of these strategies? People like to be around people like themselves. They feel comfortable in familiar, predictable patterns. They want to be with people who enjoy the same teaching style, have the same musical preferences, and ask the same questions about marriage, parenting, or dating—and, often, have the same skin color. The quickest, most efficient way to build a large church is to identify a segment of the population that shares a set of interests and cater to them in how you teach, sing, and foster friendships. This isn't a new trend. It's simply been assumed in much of church history." (RC, pp. 102–3)

Why do we like to be with people who share our personality traits or interests? Why do we feel comfortable in settings that are familiar? What's good about those kinds of relationships or places?

_____

_____

_____

_____

_____

_____

Why might someone choose a church that caters to his or her particular demographic? What might they miss out on if they did so?

_____

_____

_____

_____

_____

2. Church Is for Sinners

"Many today, both inside and outside the church, share the Pharisees' confusion. Isn't church for people with the right politics? Isn't church for people who have their act together? Isn't church for people who look, think, and talk like I do?

To a visitor who's unfamiliar with church, everyone else can look so happy, so success-
ful, so put together. And sometimes that's exactly the impression the church wants to leave.
But it's not what Jesus intended." (RC, p. 104)

On Sunday mornings, to honor the Lord, we often put on our best clothes and determine to be on our best behavior. But what might a first-time church visitor wrongly assume?

What might that person learn if he or she continued to attend?

"But [Jesus] said to him, 'A man once gave a great banquet and invited many. And at the time for the banquet he sent his servant to say to those who had been invited, "Come, for everything is now ready." But they all alike began to make excuses. The first said to him, "I have bought a field, and I must go out and see it. Please have me excused." And another said, "I have bought five yoke of oxen, and I go to examine them. Please have me excused." And another said, "I have married a wife, and therefore I cannot come." So the servant came and reported these things to his master. Then the master of the house became angry

and said to his servant, "Go out quickly to the streets and lanes of the city, and bring in the poor and crippled and blind and lame." And the servant said, "Sir, what you commanded has been done, and still there is room." And the master said to the servant, "Go out to the highways and hedges and compel people to come in, that my house may be filled.""" (Luke 14:16–23)

Who hosts the banquet in this story? Who issues the invitations?

_____

_____

_____

What excuses did the people make for not attending the banquet? What were their underlying priorities?

_____

_____

_____

_____

Whom did the master invite instead? Why do you think those people didn't make excuses?

_____

_____

_____

How does it encourage you to know that the Lord delights to invite strugglers and stragglers to his heavenly feast?

_____

_____

_____

_____

3. More Than Diversity

"The reason we need to rediscover the church as a fellowship of differents is because we too easily fall into the world's ideas about community. The world gives us two options. One perspective asks us to celebrate diversity by prioritizing differences in ethnicity, nationality, gender, and, increasingly, sexual orientation. This perspective trains us to feel right and good when these various identities are included in our community. A room full of faces of the same color feels wrong, even immoral." (RC, p. 105)

Where have you seen this perspective expressed?

_____

_____

_____

What is attractive about this perspective of celebrating diversity? Where are there hints of good in it? In what ways is it problematic?

_____

_____

_____

_____

_____

Collin Hansen writes, "Both perspectives create community through exclusion" (*RC*, p. 106). In what sense does this perspective unnecessarily exclude certain people?

_____

_____

_____

4. Beyond Uniformity

"A second perspective asks us to celebrate uniformity. In much of the world, you can't—or at least aren't supposed to—mix different ethnicities. You might live in a remote territory with only one economic class or ethnicity. Or in a country that practices a caste system that separates people before they're born, with no possibility of changing positions. Or in a political system that demands obedience to the state in all things, including religion. Uniformity is considered the highest value. A room where people disagree with each other over politics or their view of the world feels wrong, even immoral." (*RC*, pp. 105–6)

Where have you seen this perspective expressed?

_____

_____

_____

What is attractive about this perspective of celebrating uniformity? Where are there hints of good in it? In what ways is it problematic?

_____

_____

_____

_____

Collin Hansen writes, "Both perspectives create community through exclusion" (*RC*, p. 106). In what sense does this perspective unnecessarily exclude certain people?

_____

_____

_____

"My brothers, show no partiality as you hold the faith in our Lord Jesus Christ, the Lord of glory. For if a man wearing a gold ring and fine clothing comes into your assembly, and a poor man in shabby clothing also comes in, and if you pay attention to the one who wears the fine clothing and say, 'You sit here in a good place,' while you say to the poor man, 'You stand over there,' or, 'Sit down at my feet,' have you not then made distinctions among yourselves and become judges with evil thoughts? Listen, my beloved brothers, has not God chosen those who are poor in the world to be rich in faith and heirs of the kingdom, which he has promised to those who love him?" (James 2:1–5)

What does James tell the church not to do?

_____

_____

_____

How do the people of the church in James's example identify the rich man? How do they identify the poor man?

_____

_____

_____

_____

How do they treat the rich man? How do they treat the poor man?

_____

_____

_____

_____

What outward markers do we often use to make assumptions about others and to inform the way we treat them? What does this reveal about our priorities (see 1 Sam. 16:7)?

_____

_____

_____

_____

What characteristics do we highly prize in the church today? How does the fact that God has chosen the heirs of the kingdom (v. 5) force us to reevaluate our preferences?

_____

_____

_____

_____

"After this I looked, and behold, a great multitude that no one could number, from every nation, from all tribes and peoples and languages, standing before the throne and before the Lamb, clothed in white robes, with palm branches in their hands, and crying out with a loud voice, 'Salvation belongs to our God who sits on the throne, and to the Lamb!'" (Rev. 7:9–10)

What is diverse about the heavenly worshipers? What do they have in common?

_____

_____

_____

_____

How is this heavenly unity and diversity reflected in the earthly gathering of the local church?

_____

_____

_____

5. A Fellowship of Differents

"This kind of community, this fellowship of differents united by Christ alone, is what we need to rediscover in the church. And it's the kind of community that gets noticed by the world. It's the kind of community that threatens the world's status quo. This community is built on common love and belief in Jesus Christ." (*RC*, p. 108)

"[Jesus said,] 'A new commandment I give to you, that you love one another: just as I have loved you, you also are to love one another. By this all people will know that you are my disciples, if you have love for one another.'" (John 13:34–35)

What does Jesus command his disciples? What is the model for their love? What is the effect of mutual love in the church?

In what sense is loving other church members an act of evangelism? What characteristics of God's love do we display to the world when we love one another in the church?

_____

_____

_____

_____

_____

How have the truths in this chapter encouraged you to love the diverse members of your church?

_____

_____

_____

_____

CHAPTER 8

How Do We Love Outsiders?

Getting Started: Collin Hansen asks, "What is a church for?" (*RC*, p. 113). What answers have you heard to this question?

---

1. The Great Commission

"We start with the final words of Jesus to his disciples before he ascended to heaven, after his resurrection:

> *'[Jesus said,] "All authority in heaven and on earth has been given to me. Go therefore and make disciples of all nations, baptizing them in the name of the Father and of the Son and of the Holy Spirit, teaching them to observe all that I have commanded you. And behold, I am with you always, to the end of the age."' (Matt. 28:18–20)"*
> (*RC*, p. 115)

In the passage quoted here, who was Jesus speaking to? Who are Jesus's disciples today?

_____

_____

_____

What big-picture command does Jesus give his disciples? What two tasks does he say are essential to this mission? What promise does Jesus give those who take up his commission in the world?

_____

_____

_____

_____

How does the church fulfill the Great Commission today? In what ways does the work look different from that of Jesus's first disciples? In what ways is it essentially the same?

_____

_____

_____

_____

2. Turning Outsiders into Insiders

"What can we conclude, then, from the Great Commission about what church is for? How do insiders and outsiders relate? We can see that Jesus asked the first church leaders, the ultimate insiders, to undertake the business of turning outsiders into insiders through *conversion. That process could start within their own homes, with their children and extended families, but it would eventually extend to strangers around the world. The church must never lose sight of this evangelistic calling. Whatever else the church does, it teaches and then models how to become a disciple of Jesus Christ." (RC, p. 117)*

When it comes to the church, who are the "insiders"? What is their spiritual condition?

_____

_____

_____

_____

Who are the "outsiders"? What is their spiritual condition?

_____

_____

_____

_____

Why might it be unpopular to declare that certain people are "outsiders" while others are "insiders"?

_____

_____

_____

Why is it important, nonetheless, for the church to acknowledge that there are "outsiders"? What is our great hope for outsiders?

_____

_____

_____

_____

_____

"[Jesus said,] 'But you will receive power when the Holy Spirit has come upon you, and you will be my witnesses in Jerusalem and in all Judea and Samaria, and to the end of the earth.'" (Acts 1:8)

What does Jesus call his disciples to be? What does a witness do?

_____

_____

_____

What had the disciples witnessed? What have we witnessed?

_____

_____

_____

Where does Jesus say the disciples will testify about him? Why do you think Jesus begins by mentioning Jerusalem and then extending outward?

_____

_____

_____

_____

_____

_____

How did the disciples fulfill this command? How do we continue to fulfill it today?

_____

_____

_____

Who did Jesus promise to send to help the disciples? How does it encourage you in disciple-making to know that the Spirit is your helper?

_____

_____

_____

_____

_____

_____

"And Peter said to them, 'Repent and be baptized every one of you in the name of Jesus Christ for the forgiveness of your sins, and you will receive the gift of the Holy Spirit. For the promise is for you and for your children and for all who are far off, everyone whom the Lord our God calls to himself.'" (Acts 2:38–39)

Shortly after Jesus commissioned his disciples and ascended to heaven, Peter preached to the crowds at Pentecost. List the similarities between Peter's words and the directives of the Great Commission (Matt. 28:18–20). List the similarities between Peter's words and Jesus's command at his ascension (Acts 1:8).

_____

_____

_____

_____

_____

_____

_____

How have you seen the Spirit use the gospel promises to change your own life? To change the lives of your children or the people nearest to you? To change the lives of people throughout the world?

_____

_____

_____

_____

_____

How does it encourage you in disciple-making to know that it is the Lord who calls people to himself?

_____

_____

_____

_____

3. Relationships of Depth and Endurance

"We can see that a church must build relationships of depth and endurance. It's impossible to teach everything Jesus commanded to people you barely know and hardly see. Compared to previous centuries, furthermore, the difficulty of teaching everything Jesus commanded takes even more time today since, in the West at least, we've returned to a state of religious confusion closer to what the disciples would have encountered." (RC, p. 118)

Why is it important for us to develop deep and enduring relationships with our unbelieving neighbors? What are some ways we can do this? In what ways should we guard our hearts as we spend time with unbelievers?

_____

_____

_____

_____

_____

What are the fundamental truths of the gospel? Which of these (if any) do you think your non-Christian neighbors or coworkers understand?

_____

_____

_____

_____

In what ways is the task of disciple-making in your community different than it was ten years ago? Fifty years ago? A hundred years ago? In what ways is it the same?

_____

_____

_____

_____

_____

_____

4. Teaching All That Jesus Commanded

"Yes, conversion makes outsiders into insiders. But the new insiders then must learn to 'observe' Jesus's teaching." (RC, p. 117)

"When those outsiders become part of the church, the insiders patiently and diligently teach them to obey everything Jesus commanded." (RC, pp. 119–20)

In your church, what opportunities does a new convert have to learn about the life of faith?

_____

_____

_____

How are you helping others learn to obey Jesus's commands?

_____

_____

_____

5. A City Set on a Hill

"That's what happens when a church obeys the commands of Jesus together. The commands to forsake anger. To reject lust. To love enemies. To give to the needy. To not be anxious about anything. When Christians inside act this way toward one another and toward outsiders, the world sees their good works as a city set on a hill and illuminated with the twinkling lights of Christmas. Their light shines in such a way that outsiders want to come inside and give glory to the Father in heaven." (RC, p. 121)

"[Jesus said,] 'You are the light of the world. A city set on a hill cannot be hidden. Nor do people light a lamp and put it under a basket, but on a stand, and it gives light to all in the house. In the same way, let your light shine before others, so that they may see your good works and give glory to your Father who is in heaven.'" (Matt. 5:14–16)

When Jesus says, "You are the light of the world," to whom is he speaking (see vv. 1–2)? To whom does this description apply today?

_____

_____

Why is a hill a good place for a city and a stand a good place for a lamp? How is the church like a city and a lamp? What are our good works that are visible to the world?

_____

_____

When the church community lives out the gospel, what result does Jesus say we can expect (v. 16)?

How do these verses encourage you to pursue holiness?

CHAPTER 9

Who Leads?

Getting Started: Think of a pastor or elder who helped you grow spiritually. What things did he do or say that made an impact on you?

_____

_____

_____

_____

_____

_____

1. A Time of Job Training

"The short description of a pastor's job is that he is to equip you to do your job. . . . The weekly church gathering, then, is a time of job training. It allows those in the office of pastor to equip those in the office of member to know the gospel, to live by the gospel, to protect the church's gospel witness, and to extend the gospel's reach into one another's lives and among outsiders. If Jesus tasks members with affirming and building up one another in the gospel, he tasks pastors with training them to do this. If the pastors don't do their jobs well, neither will the members." (RC, pp. 126, 127)

In what specific ways do your pastors equip you and the other members of your church "to know the gospel, to live by the gospel, to protect the church's gospel witness, and to extend the gospel's reach"?

_____

_____

_____

_____

2. Equipping by Teaching

"A pastor's or elder's ministry of equipping centers on his teaching and his life." (RC, p. 128)

Western societies commonly elevate certain people for their beauty, athletic ability, charisma, connections, or wealth. What is different about the requirements for being an elder in Christ's church?

_____

_____

_____

_____

What do these God-given requirements teach us about the priorities of God's kingdom?

_____

_____

_____

_____

"And every day, in the temple and from house to house, they did not cease teaching and preaching that the Christ is Jesus." (Acts 5:42)

When did the apostles teach and preach? Where did they teach and preach? What did they teach and preach?

_____

_____

_____

_____

In what ways does the apostles' conduct in these verses provide a model for pastors and elders today?

_____

_____

_____

_____

"The saying is trustworthy: If anyone aspires to the office of overseer, he desires a noble task. Therefore an overseer must be above reproach, the husband of one wife, sober-minded, self-controlled, respectable, hospitable, able to teach, not a drunkard, not violent but gentle, not quarrelsome, not a lover of money. He must manage his own household well, with all dignity keeping his children submissive, for if someone does not know how to manage his own household, how will he care for God's church? He must not be a recent convert, or he may become puffed up with conceit and fall into the condemnation of the devil. Moreover,

he must be well thought of by outsiders, so that he may not fall into disgrace, into a snare of the devil." (1 Tim. 3:1–7)

List the things that ought to be true of an overseer (or elder).

_____

_____

_____

_____

_____

List the things that ought *not* to be true of an overseer (or elder).

_____

_____

_____

_____

Which of these things are expected of all Christians? Which are particular to the office of elder?

_____

_____

_____

_____

What is the process for selecting elders in your local church? How do these verses inform that process?

_____

_____

_____

_____

_____

_____

3. Advantages of a Plurality

"A plurality of elders has a number of benefits:

- It balances pastoral weakness. *No pastor has every gift. Other godly men will have complementary gifts, passions, and insights.*
- It adds pastoral wisdom. *None of us is omniscient.*
- It defuses an 'us vs. him' mentality *that can sometimes arise between a church and the pastor.*
- It indigenizes leadership *in the congregation, so that, even if a staff pastor leaves, the congregation still possesses a solid bulwark of leadership.*
- It creates a clear discipleship trajectory *for the men in the church. Not every man will be called by God to serve as an elder. But every man should ask himself,* Why wouldn't I serve, and do what it takes to become the kind of man who serves the body in this way? *It's good to so aspire, Paul says* (1 Tim. 3:1).
- It also sets an example of discipleship for women. *Older women in the faith should give themselves to discipling the younger women, just as elders do for the whole congregation* (Titus 2:3–4)." (*RC*, p. 133)

How have you seen these benefits in your local church? Are there other benefits that *you* would add?

_____

_____

_____

_____

_____

"The next day Moses sat to judge the people, and the people stood around Moses from morning till evening. When Moses' father-in-law saw all that he was doing for the people, he said, 'What is this that you are doing for the people? Why do you sit alone, and all the people stand around you from morning till evening?' And Moses said to his father-in-law, 'Because the people come to me to inquire of God; when they have a dispute, they come to me and I decide between one person and another, and I make them know the statutes of God and his laws.' Moses' father-in-law said to him, 'What you are doing is not good. You and the people with you will certainly wear yourselves out, for the thing is too heavy for you. You are not able to do it alone.' . . . [So] Moses chose able men out of all Israel and made them heads over the people, chiefs of thousands, of hundreds, of fifties, and of tens. And they judged the people at all times. Any hard case they brought to Moses, but any small matter they decided themselves." (Ex. 18:13–18, 25–26)

What was Moses doing?

_____

_____

_____

What problem did his father-in-law identify? What two parties were going to suffer if things continued in the same way?

_____

_____

_____

What solution did they implement?

_____

_____

_____

What can this story teach us about our need for a plurality of pastors and elders in the church?

_____

_____

_____

_____

4. What about Deacons?

"In addition to pastors/elders and members, the New Testament recognizes one other office: deacons. Deacons aren't a second body of decision makers, like some sort of bicameral legislature with the House of Representatives counterbalancing the Senate. Rather, God

gives deacons to do three things: spot and serve tangible needs, protect and promote church unity, and serve and support the ministry of the elders." (RC, pp. 136–37)

What are some situations where people with different responsibilities work side by side for a common goal?

_____

_____

_____

_____

In those situations, why is it important to delineate each party's unique responsibilities? What generally happens if it isn't clear what each party is supposed to do?

_____

_____

_____

_____

Why is it important for the church to distinguish between the responsibilities of elders and deacons?

_____

_____

_____

_____

_____

"Now in these days when the disciples were increasing in number, a complaint by the Hellenists arose against the Hebrews because their widows were being neglected in the daily distribution. And the twelve summoned the full number of the disciples and said, 'It is not right that we should give up preaching the word of God to serve tables. Therefore, brothers, pick out from among you seven men of good repute, full of the Spirit and of wisdom, whom we will appoint to this duty. But we will devote ourselves to prayer and to the ministry of the word.'" (Acts 6:1–4)

What was the problem in the church? What solution did the apostles propose? Why did they not offer to do the work themselves?

_____

_____

_____

_____

_____

How did these first deacons meet tangible needs? How did they promote unity? How did they support the elders?

_____

_____

_____

_____

_____

_____

In what specific ways do the deacons in your church fulfill the duties of their office?

_____

_____

_____

_____

What is the process for selecting deacons in your local church? How do these verses inform that process?

_____

_____

_____

_____

_____

5. The Gift of Church Leaders

"Praise God for the gifts of both elders and deacons. As you rediscover church, we hope that word sticks in your mind—gifts. God loves you, and he has given you these gifts: elders and deacons. Do you view them as gifts? Do you thank God for them as gifts? You can. They do what they do for your good and the advance of the gospel." (*RC*, p. 138)

Ask yourself the questions in the above passage. What do your answers reveal about where you need to seek the Spirit's help?

_____

_____

_____

_____

"Obey your leaders and submit to them, for they are keeping watch over your souls, as those who will have to give an account. Let them do this with joy and not with groaning, for that would be of no advantage to you." (Heb. 13:17)

In this verse, what does the Lord command us to do?

_____

_____

_____

_____

What is our church leaders' responsibility? To whom will they have to "give an account"?

_____

_____

_____

Why is it good for leaders to learn to submit to one another? If a man cannot submit to his fellow leaders or to the godly questions and corrections of a church member, why is he unsuited to lead?

_____

_____

_____

_____

How will our obedience be good for our leaders? How will it be good for us?

_____

_____

_____

What truths in this chapter encourage you to rediscover the gift of your church leaders?

_____

_____

_____

_____

You Don't Get the Church You Want, but Something Better

Questions for Personal Reflection

1. How would you describe the church you want? How would you describe the church you need? What can you learn from the differences between your answers?

---

2. What is formative about the church? How have the truths in this book helped you rediscover the value of being shaped by the church—even when it's uncomfortable?

---

3. What is beautiful about the church? How have the truths in this book helped you rediscover the loveliness of the church?

---

4. Why is the church essential? How have the truths in this book helped you rediscover the importance of showing up and helping out?

THE GOSPEL **COALITION**

The Gospel Coalition (TGC) supports the church in making disciples of all nations, by providing gospel-centered resources that are trusted and timely, winsome and wise.

Guided by a Council of more than 40 pastors in the Reformed tradition, TGC seeks to advance gospel-centered ministry for the next generation by producing content (including articles, podcasts, videos, courses, and books) and convening leaders (including conferences, virtual events, training, and regional chapters).

In all of this we want to help Christians around the world better grasp the gospel of Jesus Christ and apply it to all of life in the 21st century. We want to offer biblical truth in an era of great confusion. We want to offer gospel-centered hope for the searching.

Join us by visiting TGC.org so you can be equipped to love God with all your heart, soul, mind, and strength, and to love your neighbor as yourself.

TGC.org

 9Marks

Building Healthy Churches

9Marks exists to equip church leaders with a biblical vision and practical resources for displaying God's glory to the nations through healthy churches.

To that end, we want to see churches characterized by these nine marks of health:

1. Expositional Preaching
2. Gospel Doctrine
3. A Biblical Understanding of Conversion and Evangelism
4. Biblical Church Membership
5. Biblical Church Discipline
6. A Biblical Concern for Discipleship and Growth
7. Biblical Church Leadership
8. A Biblical Understanding of the Practice of Prayer
9. A Biblical Understanding and Practice of Missions

Find all our Crossway titles and other resources at 9Marks.org.

For Q&A videos with the authors, visit
crossway.org/RediscoverChurchVideo.